RAC
CA

Contents

RACING CARS

By Ian Penberthy

Editor: Alan Wakeford
Series Editor: Jacqui Bailey
Designer: David Jefferis

Piccolo
A Piper Book

Early Days

Our sporting instincts have always led us into racing, whether in machines, on animals or even against other people. So it is not surprising that when the new 'horseless carriages' appeared at the end of the 19th century we very soon looked for ways of matching them against each other.

These early races were not really races at all but 'relia-bility trials'. At that time the motor car was a new invention and many people did not think it would last. Being new, it had its fair share of teething problems and often would not go very far without breaking down. The reliability trials set out to prove the motor car was a perfectly good form of transport that could be relied on to take you to the end of your

journey in relative comfort.

The very first trial took place in France in 1894, between Paris and Rouen, a distance of 127 kilometres. Many competitors broke down long before they got to the end, but the event led the way for many more similar city-to-city trials.

Below: In 1895 a race was arranged from Paris to Bordeaux and back again (a total of 1,183 kilometres. It was won by Emile Levassor in this Panhard two-seater.

As time passed the cars became more reliable and faster. Unfortunately, their improved performance was not matched by improved handling. There were many fatal accidents involving both competitors and spectators, many of whom were seeing motor cars for the very first time.

Because of these crashes, permanent motor racing **circuits** were built, and these led to the development of the pure racing car in its many different forms.

The Single-Seat Racing Car

In the early days of motor racing there were no proper racing cars. The car had only just been invented and the ones that were raced were the ones that you could buy for just travelling around in.

Those early cars were little more than carriages with engines fitted, and they were very slow, often travelling at 16 k/hr or less. They were unreliable, too, and when taking part in races or 'reliability trials' on the public roads they had to carry extra spare parts, tyres and a mechanic to fix them if anything went wrong.

As time went by, the engines of those early cars became more powerful and the manufacturers began to build special versions to take part in the long city-to-city races.

The first cars had no protective bodywork for the driver and mechanic who sat really high up. As cars were improved they were fitted with bodies that protected the occupants from the weather, but they still sat quite high. In their quest for speed, however, the car makers began to build longer, more tapered and therefore more

Right: The development of the racing car. Notice how the early cars carried spare tyres. All are two-seaters except for the Mercedes Benz W125, a very powerful, streamlined racer capable of speeds approaching 320 k/hr.

streamlined bodies. The position of the seats was also lowered so that the driver and mechanic were no longer exposed to the rushing wind.

With the building of racing circuits, the number of long road races began to drop and mechanics no longer needed to ride in the car. Instead they could remain in the **pits** with a complete kit of tools and spares to service the cars while they were racing.

Because cars now only had to carry the driver it was possible to make the bodies even narrower and more streamlined. The driver was seated low down behind the engine.

From then on cars became longer, smoother and lower, and eventually the engine was moved to the back, as in modern racing cars. This spreads the weight of the car more evenly and therefore improves its handling.

Grand Prix Renault 1906

Grand Prix Benz 1908

Bugatti Type 35 1924

Mercedes Benz W125 1937

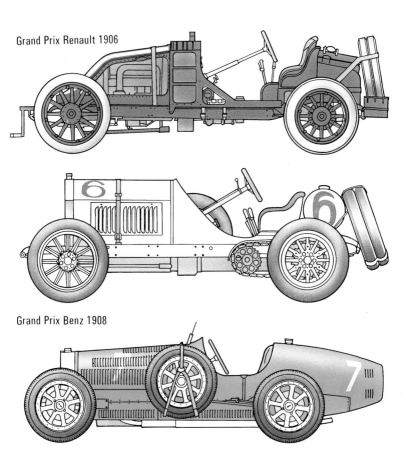

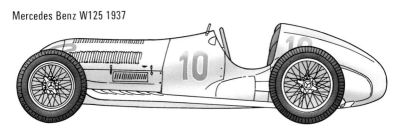

The First Racing Circuits

All the early motor races were held on public roads which until then had only ever carried horse-drawn vehicles. At first, the cars caused few problems as they did not travel fast enough to do any real damage in a crash.

It was not long, however, before the car makers began to improve the performance of their vehicles. Unfortunately, they did not always improve the brakes, steering or driver's ability to handle the extra power from the engine. Consequently, some very nasty accidents occurred.

The situation was made worse by spectators along the route who were not kept back behind barriers, and often got in the way or were hit by cars that had gone out of control. Some races even had to be stopped because of bad accidents.

This dangerous state of affairs led to sections of public roads being closed off for motor races, so forming the very first racing circuits.

Here, cars could be raced under controlled conditions and the spectators could be kept at a safe distance from them. Of course, once the race was over, the barriers were taken down and the track reverted to being public roads once more.

In 1906 the first **Grand Prix** was held at Le Mans in France where a 103-kilometre circuit had been arranged.

Closing roads off was all very well, but it meant inconvenience to the people who could no longer use them while the race was being held, and it also meant a lot of work for the organizers who had to 'build' a circuit each time they wanted to race. The answer to the problem was a permanent racing circuit and the very first of these was opened in 1907, at Brooklands in the south of England.

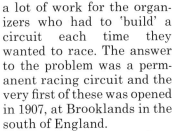

Unlike most modern racing circuits Brooklands was a **banked** track, the banking on the bends allowing the drivers to enter corners at a much faster speed than they would on a flat track. It had the added advantage of allowing spectators to see much more of the action. However, to build a banked track costs much more than making a flat circuit and very few tracks like Brooklands were built.

After Brooklands many more permanent circuits were built all over the world, but now and again public roads are still closed off to make racing circuits. Until recently, the most famous of these was in Monte Carlo where the Monaco Grand Prix was held every year.

Left: Brooklands was the first purpose-built racing circuit. During the 1920s and 1930s its banked track allowed cars to travel at very high speeds.

Formula Cars

There are many forms of motor racing and a large number of different types of racing car. But there is one type we all think of whenever the term 'racing car' is mentioned – the single-seat Formula 1 Grand Prix (GP) car. This particular type of racing car has become so well known through the international series of Grand Prix that takes place every year.

Besides the GP car there are lots of other single-seat

racing cars. They are grouped according to engine size and power output under various **'Formula'** headings – Formula 2, Formula 3, Formula Ford, etc. All are purpose-built racing cars, not developments of other forms of motor car. They all have the same basic layout and everything about them is designed for speed.

Regardless of Formula, the single-seat racing car is the most advanced of all forms of racer. A lot of high technology and engineering skill goes into its design and construction. The cars use special lightweight, strong materials, highly-tuned racing engines and other specially-made mechanical systems. Bodywork is kept to the minimum.

Driving these racing cars requires considerable skill, together with a fair degree of courage, determination and stamina. They are the cars that every racing driver hopes to race in. They provide racing in its purest form and will always be the most exciting cars to watch on the racing circuit.

The Grand Prix Car

The most sophisticated, the most powerful and the most expensive racing car is the Formula 1 Grand Prix car.

It is based on a strong but lightweight **monocoque chassis** with an aero- dynamically-styled glass fibre body and racing **independent suspension**. The car is usually fitted with a **turbocharged** 1.5-litre engine (or more rarely these days a **fuel-injected** 3-litre

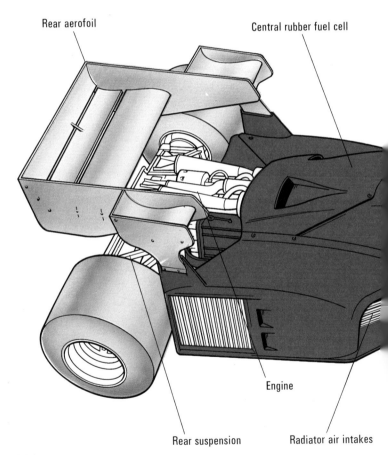

Rear aerofoil

Central rubber fuel cell

Engine

Rear suspension

Radiator air intakes

engine) producing about 600 **brake horsepower (bhp)**. This is capable of producing speeds of 320 k/hr.

Below: The modern Formula 1 car, such as this Ferrari, combines aerodynamic design with high technology.

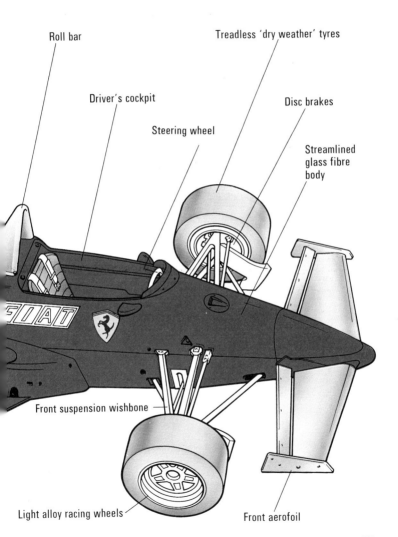

Roll bar

Treadless 'dry weather' tyres

Driver's cockpit

Disc brakes

Steering wheel

Streamlined glass fibre body

Front suspension wishbone

Light alloy racing wheels

Front aerofoil

Inside a Formula 1

Today's Formula 1 racing cars make use of a lot of aircraft construction techniques and fittings. This is done not only to get the best performance but also to ensure the car is as safe as possible when it is being raced.

Cars for Formula 1 Grand Prix racing must be built to a minimum weight limit of 580 kg. Even so, teams try to build their cars as light as possible, because the lighter the car the faster it will go. As well as being light, though, they must also be strong and this is why aircraft construction methods are used.

These days all Formula 1 cars are based around a central monocoque. This is a long narrow tub, usually made from aluminium sheet or more recently a carbon fibre material. By clever design, this tub can be made extremely strong and rigid yet still remain light in weight – much lighter than the old-fashioned tubular steel chassis that used to be fitted to Formula 1 cars.

The driver sits inside the

tub, which contains all the controls. The footwell at the front is specially strengthened to give added protection in an accident. One section is designed to absorb the impact of a head-on collision.

The front of the monocoque also carries mountings for the front suspension and steering. The back supports the engine. Behind this is a five- or six-speed **gearbox,** on either side of which are the rear suspension fittings.

Special racing **disc brakes** are fitted to the **hub** of each suspension unit.

A flexible rubber fuel tank is installed between the driver and the engine in a strong metal casing to protect it in an accident. It is connected to the engine's fuel system by short lengths of **armoured hose** with self-sealing couplings to prevent leakage of fuel if they are broken.

There are **radiators** on

Above: Formula 1 cars have lightweight removable bodies so that the pit crews can service and repair them easily.

each side of the engine and these are normally fitted inside **ducting** to direct a flow of air through them as the car moves along.

The whole car is clothed in a streamlined glass fibre body which keeps **wind resistance** to a minimum.

Aerodynamics

One of the problems with any car is that as it moves forward air is forced underneath. This air becomes very disturbed, or turbulent, as it is squeezed into the narrow space between the car's **floorpan** and the road. This causes a build up of pressure below the car. The faster the car goes, the greater the build up, until the pressure begins to push the car upwards. Consequently, the load on the tyres is reduced, which means they begin to lose their grip. This makes the car very difficult to control, particularly on bends. On a high-speed racing car this could be extremely dangerous. Apart from affecting the car's handling, the turbulent air also reduces the overall speed at which the car can travel.

To overcome the problem, racing car designers began to use the science of **aerodynamics**. They fitted **aerofoils** to both ends to provide a downforce, which overcomes the pressure as it builds up below the car. The

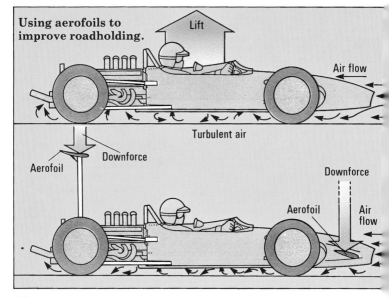

Using aerofoils to improve roadholding.

Lift

Air flow

Turbulent air

Downforce

Aerofoil

Aerofoil

Downforce

Air flow

faster the car goes, the greater the downforce, so that roadholding improves with speed.

How Aerofoils Work

An aeroplane wing works because of its shape – curved on top and flat on the bottom. As it moves forwards the air flows round it in two streams. The stream flowing over the top has to travel further than the stream below and so has to speed up. This causes a drop in pressure above the wing and this sucks the wing upwards.

If the wing is angled slightly to the air flow, the lower stream of air hits the lower surface and provides high pressure below the wing which also helps push it upwards. The faster the airflow, the greater these forces become. Turning the wing shape upside down produces the opposite effect and this is used to keep the racing car on the road.

On modern racing cars, the wings blend in much more than on early models, but you can still see them quite clearly. Indeed, the bodies are now designed to make greater use of aerodynamics and also to stop air pressure building up underneath.

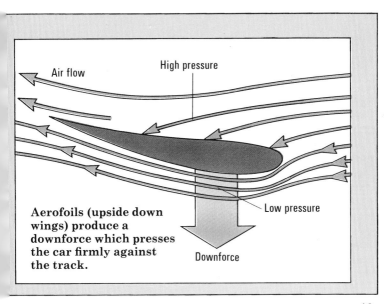

Air flow

High pressure

Low pressure

Aerofoils (upside down wings) produce a downforce which presses the car firmly against the track.

Downforce

Increasing Engine Power

Fuel Injection

Most car engines get their fuel from something called a **carburettor**. As the engine runs it draws air through this device and, in so doing, sucks petrol from tiny nozzles inside. The faster the airflow, the more petrol is sucked in, and the faster the engine runs. The driver controls the air speed with a little flap in the carburettor which is connected to the **accelerator pedal**.

This system of controlling the amount of fuel that passes to the engine is perfectly adequate for ordinary road cars. But racing cars need a more precise system known as fuel injection.

With fuel injection, the engine still sucks in the air but it flows through a simple tube (one for each of the engine's cylinders) with a nozzle at the bottom. The nozzle is connected to a pump, operated by an electronic control box which can sense the engine's speed. The pump sends a precisely measured squirt of fuel through each nozzle at exactly the right moment for the engine to run at its best at all speeds.

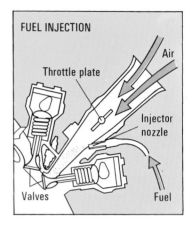

FUEL INJECTION

Air

Throttle plate

Injector nozzle

Valves

Fuel

Below: This Cosworth Ford V8 engine has eight fuel injector units on top, one for each cylinder.

Above: Notice how the turbocharger fitted to this Formula 1 car is connected into the engine's exhaust system.

called a turbocharger and it acts like a pump to force the fuel into the engine.

The turbocharger is very simple and comprises two wheels made up of blades like a fan on a common spindle. One wheel, called the turbine, is connected into the engine's exhaust system and the other (the impeller) is set in the air inlet to the engine. With the engine running,

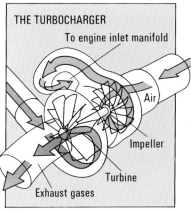

THE TURBOCHARGER
To engine inlet manifold
Air
Impeller
Turbine
Exhaust gases

The Turbocharger

Apart from fuel injection, another way an engine can be made to develop more power is to force fuel into the **combustion chambers** under pressure so that more of it is crammed in.

In recent years a device has cropped up on lots of racing cars (road cars, too) that does just that. It is

exhaust gases force the turbine to rotate and this causes the impeller to spin, pushing air along the inlet pipes where the fuel is injected. The faster the engine runs, the faster the exhaust gases spin the turbine and the quicker the impeller rotates. More and more air and fuel is therefore forced into the engine.

All About Tyres

When you look at a racing car one of the things you are bound to notice is that the tyres look different to those you would normally see on a road car. For a start they will be much wider, and there is a good chance that they will have no obvious tread pattern on them at all.

Ordinary road tyres have to cope with thousands of kilometres of motoring in all weather conditions. In contrast, racing car tyres are usually only needed for a few races (sometimes only one) so they do not have to cover long distances or have such a long life. They are also made to cope with particular weather conditions, with teams changing them as necessary, and this gives rise to their different appearance.

The job of a tyre is to transmit the power of the engine to the road to push the car along. It also has to grip the road so that the car goes where it is steered and does not slide about all over the place. The larger amount of tyre surface in contact with the road, the better it does both these jobs. With racing cars travelling so fast, drivers need to get as much

grip from the tyres as they can and that is why they are so wide.

Types of Tyre
Often, racing car tyres do not appear to have any **tread pattern**. These tyres are known as **slicks** and allow all the surface of the tyre to be in contact with the road, so producing the most amount of grip. However, they will only work when the road is dry. In the wet they ride up on a layer of water and the car goes out of control. This is known as **aquaplaning**.

For wet weather racing, teams fit treaded tyres. The grooves between the tread blocks provide an escape route for the water, allowing the rubber blocks to make contact with the road. They do not provide the same amount of grip as a slick tyre in the dry but it is good enough. Racing can therefore continue in the wet, although at slightly lower speeds. Treaded tyres of this type, however, cannot be used in dry conditions.

When weather conditions are variable it is possible to fit tyres that combine the

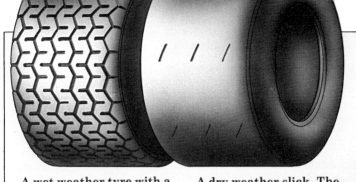

A wet weather tyre with a pronounced tread pattern.

A dry weather slick. The slits indicate the amount of tyre wear.

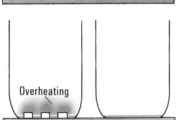

Treaded wet weather tyre

Treadless dry weather tyre

Water

Overheating

In wet weather, the treaded tyre's grooves provide an escape route for the water so the tread can grip the road. The treadless slick rides up on top of the water.

In the dry, the treadless tyre provides a large contact area for good grip, but the treaded tyre overheats and the tread flies apart.

best features of both wet and dry weather tyres.

Tyres always provide more grip when they are warm; the rubber becomes sticky. That is why you often see drivers weaving about sharply on any warm-up lap before the race begins. Doing this heats up the rubber, so the tyres are at their best from the very beginning of the race.

Soft rubber, too, provides plenty of grip. That is why special tyres made from this are often used in **qualifying sessions** to give the fastest lap times possible. But these soft tyres are not strong enough to last a whole race and so tyres made of harder compounds have to be used .

The Road to Success

For a driver to jump into a Formula 1 Grand Prix car straight from racing saloon cars would be almost suicidal. To cope with such high-performance, high technology machines drivers need to build up their experience of racing single-seat cars gradually.

At the very bottom of the ladder to that Formula 1 drive are various Formulae based on production car en-

gines and components. These allow a single-seat car to be built and run for a fraction of the cost of a Formula 1 car.

Probably best known and most popular of these is Formula Ford. These small single-seat racers make use of 1.6-litre overhead cam Ford Cortina engines which can only be modified very slightly so they do not put out too much power. The cars run on normal road tyres

allowed, as are racing tyres and aerofoils.

Other production car based forms of racing are Formula Vee and Formula SuperVee which are similar in idea to the Formula Ford types of racing, but they make use of Volkswagen engines and mechanical components.

These very simple forms of single-seat racing meet two needs. They provide a relatively inexpensive way for an enthusiast to go racing in a single-seater and they give a good start to those wishing to make a career in racing.

which is another limiting factor. Unlike their bigger cousins in the Formula 1 world, Formula Ford cars have a tubular steel chassis but they have the same sort of racing suspension and braking systems. They have glass fibre bodies, but they are not allowed aerofoils like the larger cars.

A step up from Formula Ford is Formula Ford 2000 which uses the larger 2-litre Ford engine and is a much more sophisticated form of car. More engine tuning is

There are several other forms of single-seat racing, the most notable being Formula 3 and Formula 2 which provide stepping stones to Formula 1 for many drivers. Both are scaled down Grand Prix cars and use 2-litre racing engines. The engines in Formula 3 cars only develop 160–170 bhp but those in Formula 2 cars are twice as powerful. Formula 2 cars tend to run in longer races, too, preparing their drivers for that jump into Formula 1.

Sports & Saloon Cars

Beyond the glamour of single-seat racing there is still an exciting range of other car types which are raced on circuits. These can roughly be divided into two categories – sports cars and saloon/touring cars.

Ever since the very beginnings of motor sport, people have raced the kind of cars that can be bought off the showroom floor, and today is

no exception. Depending on the class they race in, they may have virtually no changes to the condition they were in when they left the factory. Some, however, may be drastically modified and only bear a passing resemblance to their production cousins.

Some sports cars are purpose-built for racing and are not the sort of car you

would see driving on the road. These cars are intended to take part in long-distance endurance races, such as the 24-hour race which takes place at Le Mans in France every year. These cars have very low, streamlined bodies and are every bit as sophisticated as a Formula 1 racer.

Because sports and saloon car racing is so varied and the cars so different, there is something in it for everyone, both competitors and spectators alike. For competitors it can be an inexpensive way

Above: This BMW M1 racer shows how sometimes you have to look very closely for any resemblance to a factory model.

to go racing – they can often drive their racing car to the circuit, but they must be careful not to crash it during the race! For spectators it is fun to watch cars seen every day on the road racing against each other. They can cheer on the same type of cars that they perhaps own themselves.

Endurance Racing

The most exciting and impressive racing sports cars are those designed and built for endurance racing. These long distance events which last for six hours or more (the famous Le Mans race lasts for a whole day and night), are a punishing test of drivers and cars, they are far more gruelling than any other form of motor sport.

The Chevrolet Corvette (above) and the Porsche 956 (below) are typical of purpose-built endurance racers.

Each car will have two drivers who take it in turns to drive the car throughout the event, each spending about two hours at a time at the wheel. They change

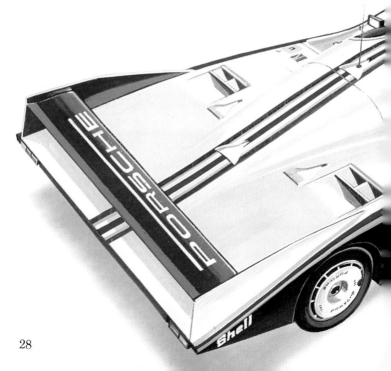

places at scheduled pit stops when fuel is topped up and tyres replaced. And although the cars all have two seats, there is only ever the driver on board during a race.

One of the most important qualities an endurance racing sports car has to have

is strength, as it will be running virtually flat out for the entire duration of the

race. All the mechanical systems of the car must be put together very carefully if they are to survive. Often the strain proves too much and engines begin to fail towards the end of the race.

Types of Car

Endurance sports cars can broadly be divided into two groups – those based on very highly modified production sports cars and those which are purpose-built, in effect racing cars with exotic, aerodynamic two-seater bodies. It is quite common for both to race in the same events.

These cars are almost always fitted with highly-tuned racing engines, racing car suspension and braking systems, lightweight bodywork and racing wheels and tyres. The purpose-built versions are often of monocoque construction like Formula 1 cars. They have similar engines (with turbochargers) and are capable of speeds of over 320 k/hr.

24 Hours at Le Mans

The 24-hour sports car endurance race which takes place at Le Mans is probably the most well known of all motor races. It has a history that goes back over 60 years, and it draws racing teams and spectators from all over the world.

Surprisingly, the circuit at Le Mans is still made each year by closing off public roads just outside the city, which is a little over 160 kilometres to the south-west of Paris. It has been this way since the very first motor race to be held there – the French Grand Prix in 1906.

The circuit has been altered many times in its life and now comprises a very testing 13.4 kilometres from start to finish. One particularly trying feature is the Mulsanne straight which ends in a sharp right-hand bend. Cars often reach speeds of 370 k/hr or so on this straight and they have to brake sharply to take the bend, putting tremendous strain on braking and suspension systems. In a short race this might not cause too much concern, but the Le Mans race lasts for a full 24 hours and the constant ac-

celeration and braking takes its toll on the cars. It is not unusual for more than half of the cars not to finish!

The race normally takes place in June, beginning at 4 pm on a Saturday and running through to 4 pm on the following Sunday. All through the afternoon, night and following morning, the

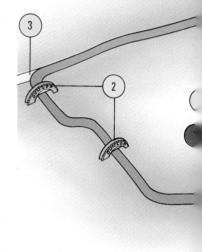

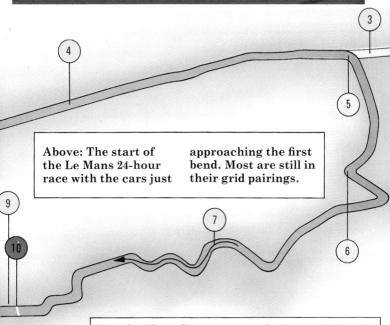

Above: The start of the Le Mans 24-hour race with the cars just approaching the first bend. Most are still in their grid pairings.

Key: Le Mans Circuit
1. Start
2. Dunlop bridges
3. Public roads to Le Mans and Tours
4. Mulsanne straight
5. Mulsanne corner
6. Indianapolis bends
7. Cars' direction of travel
8. Race control
9. Pits and viewing balconies
10. Finish

Above: Racing at Le Mans during the early 1950s. Notice the early form of start and the leisurely pit stop by an Aston Martin.

cars thunder round the track, flames licking from their turbochargers as they decelerate for the bends. Hurried pit stops are made to change drivers, take on fuel and make vital repairs that will keep the cars running just a little while longer. There is a very exciting atmosphere about the whole circuit, with spectators willing their favourite cars to keep going.

Early Days

Although some of the early French Grand Prix races were held at Le Mans, it was not until 1923 that the first endurance event was held there. The original purpose of the race was to provide a real test for normal road-going touring cars. These powerful open cars had folding canvas tops, two or four

seats and had to compete with all their normal road equipment. Indeed, one purpose of the race was to test all this equipment to see if it would stand up to a long spell of rigorous motoring.

Originally at the start, the teams had to put up the cars' tops before the drivers could pull away into the race. But as the years progressed and more and more sports cars with solid roofs took part a new starting method was found. All the cars were lined up on one side of the track with their drivers facing them on the opposite side. When the starter dropped the flag, the drivers had to run across the track, jump into their cars, start them up and pull away into the race. Sadly this exciting way of starting a race is now considered too dangerous and a normal **grid** system is used instead.

Super Saloons

Part of the fun of watching motor racing is in picking a car to follow to see how it does against the opposition. It is even more fun if the car you pick looks like the one your family owns, and with saloon car racing you can do just that.

The cars taking part are based on the kind of cars you see every day on the road. In some cases they are almost exactly the same, but at other times you have to look very hard to see the resemblance.

As with all forms of racing, drivers and teams always want to make their cars go

faster and faster, and to do this they have to make more and more mechanical changes and alterations to the bodywork. To prevent any unfair advantage, the organizers set certain limits to the amount of changes that can be made to cars in any particular class.

In the highest forms of saloon car racing, however, the modifications are so great that the cars are almost proper racing cars with saloon car bodies dropped over them. They have turbocharged racing engines, strengthened and lowered suspension to improve road-

In the higher forms of saloon and sports car racing, it is often difficult to tell just what the cars are. Above is a racing Ford Capri, below, the standard model.

holding, high-performance braking systems and proper racing tyres fitted to very wide wheels. Bodies are widened to cover the tyres and they have **spoilers** and aerofoils both to prevent air build up below the cars and to provide extra downforce when travelling at speed. Often the only way you can identify the original car is to look at them side on – or look at the grille badge!

Simple Saloons

Taking part in any form of motor racing is an expensive hobby, but there are ways of keeping the costs down. Racing a car that is not highly modified is one of them. If the car can be driven to the circuit under its own power, so much the better as the competitor will not have to buy a trailer and towing car. Saloon car racing can be just this sort of inexpensive sport.

The lower classes of saloon car racing, where you can race just about any sort of saloon car you can think of, are relatively cheap to enter. This form of racing is interesting to the spectator who can see cars like his own battling it out on the track. It is good for car makers, too, because racing is an ideal way of advertising the qualities of the cars they make. But most of all it is fun for the competitors who can go racing each weekend and keep their costs down.

One-Make Championships

There are lots of different forms of saloon car racing, but some of the most interesting are the 'one-make championships'. In these, a series of races is arranged, based on one particular make and model of car. For example there is a one-make championship for the Ford Fiesta and another for the Renault 5 Turbo. Although it may sound a boring competition in fact it produces some very exciting and close racing. As all the cars are the same, with the same amount of modifications allowed, they are all evenly matched. This means that races are won on the skill of the driver and not on who can build the most powerful and best handling car. These one-make championships are a good way to get into motor racing and they are well supported.

The Pre-1957 Series

Another form of low-budget saloon car racing is the Pre-1957 series. This is a series of races for cars built before 1957. For anyone interested in older cars, it is a treat to see these restored models racing each other on the circuit. In many cases these cars are not old enough to be sought after by collectors and would be destined for the scrap heap. Racing them gives them a new lease of life and it gives their drivers a chance to have a go at racing without being too much out of pocket.

Right: Saloon car racing also includes events for older models like this Jaguar.

Below: Saloon car racing is often as exciting and colourful as the more exotic forms of motor sport.

US Stock Car Racing

In America the term 'stock' means standard or production, and **stock car** racing in America, unlike Europe, means production saloon car racing. However, these large, high-performance saloons are far from standard. They have highly-tuned engines of 5.8 litres, specially designed lowered suspensions and uprated brakes. The interiors are stripped out and a single seat fitted for the driver.

The other unusual thing about American stock car racing is that it takes place on banked oval tracks and the races are often long distance affairs – 500 miles (800 kilometres) is common. This means that the drivers have to race for anything up to four hours and they have to make regular pit stops to take on more fuel and replace tyres.

The cars are very powerful and are capable of 320 k/hr on the straight. At the famous Daytona track – a 2½-mile (4-kilometre) oval – the cars have to do 200 laps to complete the race. Average lap speeds of over 240 k/hr

Above: American stock cars are highly modified modern saloon cars.

Below: Banked oval tracks, such as Daytona, are used for stock car racing in America.

are common. It is a very exciting close form of racing.

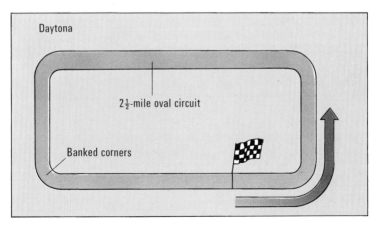

Daytona

2½-mile oval circuit

Banked corners

Short-Circuit Racing

All forms of motor racing are exciting to watch, but one problem that faces spectators at many events is that they simply cannot see the whole race from where they are standing or sitting. This is because road circuits twist and snake around and much of the race takes place out of sight. However, there is one form of racing you can watch from start to finish – short-circuit racing.

Short-circuit tracks take the form of a small, narrow oval with raised terraces all round for spectators.

The three main types of car that race on these oval tracks are stock cars, hot rods and bangers. Because the tracks are short and narrow, racing is often fast and furious with plenty of thrills and spills.

Stock Cars

Probably the most spectacular form of short-cicuit racing is stock car racing because the drivers are encouraged to push and shove each other out of the way when they want to pass. This results in some spectacular action with cars sliding

and spinning across the track, tipping over and sometimes even flying through the

Below: This Formula 1 stock car has an American Chevrolet V8 engine. Notice the strong tubular steel bumpers and side guards.

air! Thankfully, the cars have a strong chassis with reinforced bumpers and side guards, and the drivers are well protected with steel **roll-over cages** and strong harnesses, so there is seldom any serious damage done to either cars or drivers.

The earliest stock cars, which appeared just over thirty years ago, were little more than stripped down and strengthened old jalopies. In fact the term 'stock' means standard, but now they are purpose-built single-seat racing cars with highly tuned engines and sophisticated suspension systems, although sometimes they may look a little battered on the outside. The most powerful are the **Formula 1 stock cars** which have American V8 engines.

Hot Rods

The most sophisticated form of short-circuit racing car is the **hot rod**. Unlike stock cars and bangers, both of which smash into each other in the course of a race, hot rod drivers rely on their speed and skill to get past each other.

The hot rod is really a short-circuit version of the normal circuit-racing saloon car. It is based on a small, modern saloon bodyshell with all the windows removed and a strong roll cage inside to protect the driver should the car roll over. It has a lowered and stiffened racing suspension system, uprated braking and steering systems and a highly-tuned full-race engine. Racing tyres on wide alloy wheels complete the package.

Hot rods are very fast and manoevrable and on the short oval tracks (often less than 0.5 kilometre from start to finish) they produce some very exciting close racing as the opportunities for passing are few and far between.

42

Above: These Ford Escort hot rods are the short-circuit version of normal circuit racing saloon cars.

Unlike racing on a full size circuit, the field of cars does not get strung out so they are always in contact with each other.

One reason the racing is particularly furious is that the fastest drivers start the race at the back of the grid rather than at the front as in most other forms of racing. In short-circuit racing there is no qualifying session to determine grid placings. Instead a points grading system based on the driver's performance in previous meetings fixes the starting positions. The points are totalled up throughout the racing season month by month and each month drivers have to paint the roof of their cars a certain colour to match the points they hold.

Novice drivers and low points scorers have white roofs and start at the front of the grid, the next grade have yellow roofs, followed by cars with blue roofs and finally the fastest drivers and highest points holders with red roofs. The World Champion has a gold roof and has to start behind everybody else.

This is quite a fair system as it means the beginners get a good start and a chance to gain some experience, while the more experienced, faster racers really have to prove how good they are, not only by beating each other but by working their way right through the field to the front every time they enter a race.

Like most short-circuit cars, hot rods are very colourful and are usually the smartest turned out.

Race to Destruction!

If hot rods are the most sophisticated form of short-circuit racer, **bangers** are at the opposite end of the scale. They were introduced to provide a particularly cheap form of motor racing that anyone could get into and that would provide a lot of fun for both racers and spectators alike.

Bangers are old cars that have come to the end of their useful lives on the road and are usually only fit for the scrapyard. But with a bit of fixing up, the windows taken out, a safety harness and usually a roll cage welded in, they can provide a cheap racing car ideal for the short-circuit.

Banger drivers are encouraged to bump and shove each other as they race together, and being just road cars with no extra strengthening, they soon become very bashed about – bonnets and boot lids fall off, wings are pushed in, but they still keep racing, often with jets of steam hissing from broken radiators.

Usually a short-circuit meeting will have two or three banger races with a **demolition derby** at the end In this race all the bangers that can still run are raced

together, the last one still moving being declared the winner. The drivers ram each other in their cars, hoping to eliminate the opposition, yet still keep going themselves. They often do this by reversing into other cars to prevent

damaging their own steering and engine at the front of the car.

Bangers are often raced in teams, each team working together to remove the opposition before starting on each other!

Below: Banger racing is a popular form of short-circuit racing because it is cheap and because the spectators enjoy seeing the cars crash furiously into one another. . It makes use of old, worn-out cars that would otherwise go to the scrapyard.

Karting

Of all the forms of four-wheeled motor sport, karting is the only one in which youngsters can take part. If you are 11 or older you can get a **kart** racing licence and go racing. In fact, lots of drivers get their first taste of competition in karts. Many stay with the sport, but others often move on to racing full-size cars, sometimes with great success. Several top racing drivers 'cut their teeth' on these little racers.

Kart racing is exciting, not just for the spectators but for the racers themselves. Karts are fast – many will do over 160 k/hr – and being so close to the ground the drivers really get a sensation of speed. They are very safe, too, but drivers are required to wear tough clothing (like motorcycle racers) and helmets so that even if an accident does happen there is the least possible chance of serious injuries.

Karts are raced in several different types of event, but the main ones are short circuit (not an oval like a stock car track but a miniature twisting track about 1.2 kilo-

metres long) and long circuit (often full-size car circuits).

A short-circuit race is usually divided into a number of ten-lap heats, the karts beginning the race from a rolling start. They form up in their grid positions and then do one or two warm-up laps at slow speed. When the starter is happy that they are all in position he waves them away as they come round to the start line to begin the

first of their ten laps.

Points are awarded to drivers depending on their placings at the end of each heat and these points determine the grid positions in the next heat. When all the heats have been run, the points are totalled up and the driver with the most is declared the winner.

In a long-circuit event there is usually a time limit and the winner is the one

Above: Racing karts is fun. These are Superkarts fighting for position in a close fought race. Look how small they are, but they are very fast.

who has completed the most laps when the time is up.

Karts are also raced on other forms of track as well, sometimes short ovals and even on ice in colder parts of the world.

Types of Kart

The very first karts appeared about thirty years ago in America. They were little more than a tubular frame, four small wheels, a seat and a lawnmower engine. But they have changed a lot since then, and though the very basic modern kart may still look very similar to those early versions, it is much more sophisticated and much faster.

The simplest karts are used in short-circuit racing. They have a lightweight tubular frame with an upright seat for the driver. The air-cooled motorcycle-type engine is behind the seat and drives the back axle – there is no gearbox or **clutch** which is why they have to make a **rolling start**. They

Right: Superkarts have streamlined bodies and aerofoils which improve their speed and roadholding.

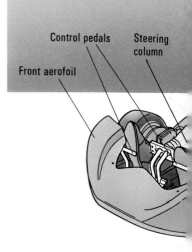

Control pedals

Steering column

Front aerofoil

Below: This kart has a rocket engine and can travel at over 320 k/hr!

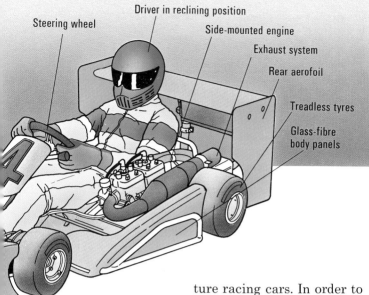

Steering wheel

Driver in reclining position

Side-mounted engine

Exhaust system

Rear aerofoil

Treadless tyres

Glass-fibre
body panels

cannot remain stationary with the engine running. The fuel tank is also behind the seat.

In front of the driver is a small steering wheel linked to the front axle and two pedals – an accelerator and a brake pedal. The kart has lightweight alloy racing wheels and special treadless racing tyres for dry conditions or treaded tyres for the wet. There is no suspension, and the brakes only work on the rear wheels.

Long-circuit karts are much more sophisticated, some of them resemble minia-ture racing cars. In order to reduce wind resistance, the drivers almost lay down in their karts and the engine is mounted next to them. Fuel tanks, too, are fitted along each side. They have clutches, gearboxes and four-wheel braking systems. Engines in these karts can be up to 250 cc, making them very fast.

Many long-circuit karts have bodywork to smooth the flow of air over their frames and so reduce wind resistance even more. Like full-size racing cars they have aerofoils to improve handling. Formula E karts have full bodies that enclose the driver completely.

Dragsters

Although most forms of motor racing take place on a circuit of some kind, there is one sport, drag racing, where the track is laid out in a straight line. It is only a quarter of a mile long (just under half a kilometre) and pairs of cars are raced along it in a knock-out competition, which is known as an **elimination**.

Prior to racing, the cars take part in a qualifying session where they are raced against the clock. Then the quickest, say, 16 are split into pairs and raced against each other in the first round of the elimination. The winner from each pair goes through to the second round and so on until there is an overall winner.

Drag racing is a severe test of both driver and car. The drivers must have very sharp reactions, and be able to control their cars instinctively and cope with high **G-forces**. Some cars accelerate to over 160 k/hr in a second or less. The car builders have to make sure their cars will accelerate as quickly as possible as each race only lasts a few seconds.

Classes of Drag Racing
There are many different classes of drag racing vehicle, ranging from the ultimate Top Fuel **dragsters** down to ordinary production

cars. In fact you can race practically any kind of car – or motorcycle – at a drag racing event. All have their own eliminations.

Under the Christmas Tree
Cars are started by a traffic-light system called the **Christmas Tree** because of its coloured lights. A series of amber lights count down to the green 'go' light, and if the car crosses the start line before this comes on, a red light flashes and it is disqualified.

Light beams shone across the track at the start and finish operate electronic timing equipment when the cars pass through them. The equipment shows which car crossed the finish line first,

Above: All manner of cars are used for drag racing. Some have quite novel designs.

Below: Because racing fuels are highly flammable and poisonous, drivers of front-engined cars wear flame-proof masks.

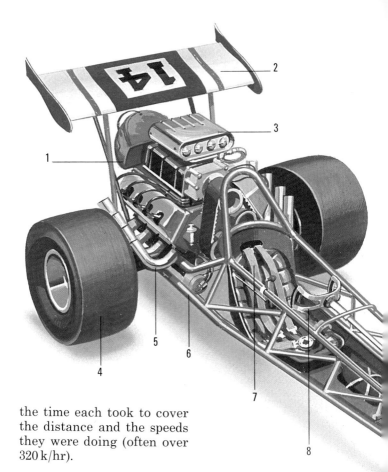

the time each took to cover
the distance and the speeds
they were doing (often over
320 k/hr).

The Top Fuel Dragster

The quickest drag racing
vehicles are the pure dragsters – cars designed with
one aim in mind; to cover the
quarter mile in the shortest
possible time. And the most
powerful of these are the Top
Fuel dragsters.

Top Fuel dragsters have
the largest engines permitted
and they run on a special fuel
mixture of nitromethane and
methanol which allows the
engines to produce much
more power than if they were
running on normal petrol.

Cars such as this can cover
the quarter mile from a standing start in $5\frac{1}{2}$ seconds and
be doing nearly 420 k/hr as
they cross the finish line.

Key:
1. Braking parachute
2. Rear aerofoil applies downwards pressure on the rear tyres for maximum grip
3. Fuel-injected, supercharged V8 engine developing 2,000 bhp
4. Low-pressure, treadless 'slick' tyres ensure maximum contact with the track
5. Exhaust pipes or 'headers'
6. Lightweight tubular frame just wide enough for the engine and driver. The long, tapered frame helps keep the car in a straight line at speed
7. Driver's safety harness
8. Special twin-grip steering wheel often known as a 'butterfly tiller'
9. Crash helmet
10. Flameproof overalls
11. Steering column
12. Fuel tank holding just enough fuel for one race
13. Front aerofoil helps keep the front tyres on the ground at high speeds to aid steering
14. Lightweight, spoked motorcycle front wheels with aluminium trims to ensure timing light beams are broken at the finish line

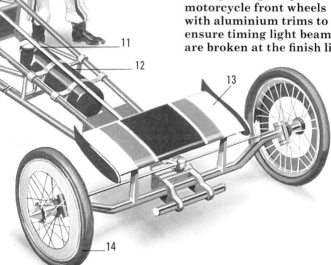

The Powerhouse

The engine is the heart of any drag racing car, and designers cram the largest, most powerful engine they can find into the lightest frame they can build so that the car will travel as quickly as possible over the quarter mile track.

These engines are not like any you will find in a road car. They have over four times the capacity of the average family car engine and 30 times the power.

Unlike engines in circuit racing cars which are required to run for long periods

of time and at a wide range of speeds, the drag racing engine only runs for short periods at a time (one or two minutes at the most). And it has to run flat-out from start to finish. This puts a tremendous strain on the engine so it must be strengthened internally. However, as it only has to run for a short time, it can be tuned to give much more power than if it had to last a long circuit race. This is done with special pistons, valves, cylinder heads, cam shafts and fuel systems.

Left: A typical dragster engine is based on an American V8 and is supercharged to obtain the most power.

The most popular engines for dragsters are eight-cylinder engines taken from big American cars and re-built. But the really fast cars have specially-made aluminium versions which produce even more power and save weight.

The power the engine develops depends on how much fuel can be forced into its combustion chambers – the more fuel fed in, the more power. So the most powerful dragster engines are always fitted with a **supercharger** which acts like a big pump to force the fuel into the engine. Often, the supercharger is fitted with fuel injection as well (see pages 20–21).

Some engines run on normal petrol, but the most powerful use special racing fuels such as methanol and nitromethane which allow the engine to develop much more power – sometimes too much and the engine will blow up in a spectacular explosion.

Below: The supercharger forces fuel into the engine like a turbocharger, but being driven by a belt from the engine it reacts instantly to changes in speed whereas the turbocharger lags behind a little.

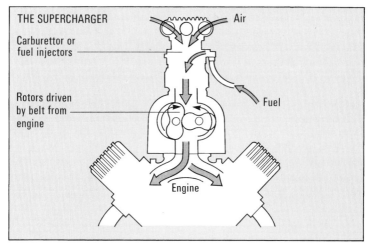

THE SUPERCHARGER

Carburettor or fuel injectors

Rotors driven by belt from engine

Air

Fuel

Engine

From Street to Strip

Drag racing began in America during the 1930s and 1940s when cars were raced on main streets or 'drags'. Eventually the authorities made old disused airfields available to these early 'hot rodders' and the first drag racing strips were born. Very soon, what had been an illegal and very dangerous form of racing became a very respectable and professional motor sport.

Burnouts, Wheelies and Parachutes

Drag racing is a contest of acceleration and to get the best acceleration from the car, the tyres must grip the track as much as possible so

Above: Drag racing is an acceleration test. This Altered is doing a wheelie.

that every little bit of power is used to push the car forwards.

If the tyres are cold they will not grip the track well enough and the wheels will spin, slowing down the car. To overcome this, the drag racer usually does a **'burnout'** before the race. A little water is poured on to the track in front of each rear tyre, the car rolled forwards into the puddles and then the throttle opened. The smooth slick tyres will not grip the track at all through the water and so they spin furiously, generating a lot of friction. This heats up the rubber and makes it very sticky so that when the car races its tyres really grip well. A lot of smoke from burning rubber adds to the drama of the burnout.

Sometimes the tyres grip so well that they will not move at all, and the rear axle rotates instead, causing the front of the car to lift off the track in a **'wheelie'**.

In order to get the most amount of grip or 'traction' at the rear tyres, cars are built with most of their weight towards the rear. One weight-saving ploy at the front of the car is to remove the front brakes and use very light front wheels and tyres.

Because the rear brakes would not be capable of stopping a really fast car on their own, the most powerful drag-racing cars have parachutes fixed to the back. The driver releases the parachute to provide extra braking force as he crosses the finish line and cuts the power.

Below: Two drag-racing Funny Cars doing burnouts to warm their tyres before racing each other. Notice the clouds of rubber smoke. You can also see the 'Christmas Tree' starting equipment between them.

Rallying

Probably the oldest form of motor sport is the rally. Yet rallying is not really racing although it may seem as though it is. Instead, it is a sort of time trial. The route of each rally is broken up into a number of sections and drivers are given a time by which they must reach the end of each part. If they are late then they are penalized.

Unlike a normal motor race when all the cars start together, in a rally the cars are started individually at one minute intervals. If they all took the right amount of time to cover the section, they would all arrive at one

minute intervals, but this rarely happens.

However, it is possible for more than one car to complete all the sections in the time allowed and that would give more than one winner. To overcome this problem, all rallies include sections where the cars have to cover the distance as fast as possible and the results are used to help find the winner.

Another way in which a

rally differs from a normal motor race is that all the cars carry a navigator whose job is to guide the driver along the route so that he does not have to worry about finding his own way and can concentrate on driving as fast as possible.

Types of Rally

There are two types of rally: the road rally and the stage rally. Road rallies take place entirely on public roads (quite often at night to avoid annoying the public) and may cover hundreds of kilometres. Stage rallies, on the other hand, take place on private roads, farm tracks, disused airfields and even motor racing circuits. On stage rallies, the drivers have to complete each stage as quickly as possible. Sometimes all the stages are in one place, but at some events they are spread over a large area of the countryside and the cars have to be driven on public roads from one stage to the next.

Left: Rally cars often have to cope with rough conditions. Here, a car on the Safari Rally in Africa is crossing a shallow river. It carries spare tyres like the earliest racing cars.

The Rally Story

In a sense the very first motor races at the turn of the century could be considered rallies. As in rallies, the object was to get from one place to another. The cars were started at regular timed intervals, carried a passenger (a mechanic in this case) and the crews had to navigate all of the route for themselves.

But it was in Germany in 1904 that the first 'official' rally was held. Known as the Herkomer Trial, the event had a number of control points along the route which had to be visited by the drivers in a set order, and they had to keep to strict average speeds between each control.

Other events in Austria and Germany soon followed. Then in 1911 a group of businessmen in Monte Carlo arranged the very first Monte Carlo Rally which is probably the most famous

Left: This Ford Zephyr shows just how few changes were made to cars in the 1950s before they went rallying.

rallying event in the world.

In the Monte Carlo Rally cars set off from points all over Europe heading towards Monte Carlo. And they took part in various rally stages on the way. The event was held in the winter when the weather conditions on the route could be quite severe, making it an even stiffer test of both crews and cars.

Another major milestone in rallying history came in 1929 when the first **RAC** Rally was held in Britain. The event continues to this day and is very popular with spectators and competitors alike.

Also among the famous rallies is the Safari Rally which takes place in Kenya, Africa. This is reckoned to be one of the toughest rallies there is, the cars often travelling for hundreds of kilometres without seeing a tarmac road.

In the very early days of the sport, the cars were little more than standard production models with a few extra lights added. This must have made competing particularly hazardous.

Below: This PV Volvo is negotiating a mountain road during the 1962 Monte Carlo Rally.

The Modern Rally Car

All rally cars are still based on standard production cars. But these are strengthened and modified to stand up to the punishing treatment they receive. They must also have two seats.

The suspension, braking system and steering are all uprated and the **engine tuned** to improve perform-ance. To ensure the engine and back axle are protected from damage by rocks in the road, stout metal plates are fitted underneath.

Because many rallies are held at night, the cars carry extra spotlights on the front and sometimes have a two-way radio to keep in touch with service crews.

Key: Peugeot 205 Turbo 16 Rally Car

1. Crew wear crash helmets and proper racing overalls.
2. Radio link to service crew.
3. Uprated steering, suspension and braking systems.
4. Wide-rimmed wheels with road, racing or off-road studded tyres.
5. Sponsors' decals.
6. Strong roll cage inside also reinforces body.
7. Air intake for engine radiators.
8. Four-wheel-drive transmission.
9. Mid-mounted, turbocharged engine.
10. Rear portion of body tilts upwards to expose engine and transmission for maintenance, tuning, etc.

Rally Stages

One of the drawbacks of a normal road rally is that there are lots of restrictions on the competitors. One of the most important is that they keep to the normal road speed limits. These and the fact that very often it is not possible to close off public roads for a rally mean that a road rally can never really be a flat-out affair.

A stage rally, on the other hand, is totally different. Because it is held on private ground, speed restrictions can be lifted and the stages can be arranged to make the most of the natural features of the land to test the drivers' car handling skills.

There will be several stages, or short courses, in each stage rally and each one might be on a different type of surface or have different types of hazard for the crews to overcome. The length of the stage can range from as little as 1.6 kilometres to as many as 32 (1 to 20 miles). Turning points and road junctions are signposted by the organizers and the crews have to find their own way round the course as quickly as they can.

Below: Stage rallies take place on a number of private roads and tracks where cars can travel at speed safely.

Open road

Forest tracks

Tarmac tracks

If the stages of the rally are spread over a large area of the countryside, the cars are driven from one to another on the public roads. These sections are not competitive sections and the cars have to be driven at normal road speeds and obey all traffic regulations. Often the navigator and driver switch roles on these sections, to enable the driver to relax and get ready for the next stage. A stage rally might take a full

Above: Harsh conditions are common on rallies. This Escort is running on packed snow in the 1984 Swedish rally.

day to complete, or a full night.

Cars used for stage rallies must be much tougher than those used for normal road rallies as the conditions they have to cope with include forest tracks and similar unpaved routes.

The Driving Team

Although fast driving is as essential to rallying as any other form of motor sport, success in this particular sport relies on good teamwork between the driver and navigator. Drivers must drive the cars as fast as they can between one control point and the next, but as they are not on closed circuits like race tracks they must be guided in the right direction – this is the navigator's job.

Before the rally begins the navigators will be given a set of route instructions by the organizers. From these they will work out the positions of the control points on a map and the routes between the points. They will also work out the direction the car must take from point to point. In some cases they may have to do this as the car is being driven on the early parts of the course, making it a particularly tricky job.

Below: Winning in rallying depends on teamwork between the driver and navigator who share the honours.

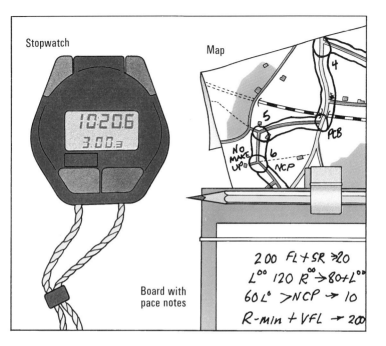

Stopwatch

Map

4

5

PCB

NO MAKE UP

6

NCP

Board with pace notes

200 FL + SR ≫20
L°° 120 R°° →80 + L°°
60 L° > NCP → 10
R-min + VFL → 200

Once the navigators have worked out the route, they have to tell the driver which turnings to go down and which direction to take at road junctions.

In some cases, rally crews are allowed to drive the course before the event, allowing the navigator to make a series of coded **pace notes**. By using their own codes and a series of symbols, navigators can cram a lot of information about the course on to a small sheet of paper. Using these notes they can then tell their drivers when to expect a sharp right- or

Above: Essential equipment for the rally navigator: stopwatch, maps and clipboard with course notes.

left-hand bend, when to expect a shallow one, when to expect a junction and so on. With this information drivers can tailor their driving technique exactly to the course requirements.

The other important jobs navigators have to carry out are the checks on time and average speed so that they can tell the driver if they are running behind or ahead of schedule.

Off-Road Racing

Off-road racing is one of the most gruelling motor sports in the world. In this sport there are no specially-prepared, smooth high-speed tracks. Instead drivers have to deal with some of the roughest conditions a vehicle ever has to go through.

Off-road events take place throughout the world, and their form depends on the local conditions available to the racers. Some are long endurance events through harsh desert conditions, such as the 1000-mile (about 1600 kilometres) Baja 1000 race through Mexico.

The object of off-road racing is to pit both drivers and machines against each

Below: Four-wheel-drive vehicles like these American pickup trucks are popular for off-road events.

Right: The route of the famous Baja 1000 race through Mexico.

other and against the terrain: it may be desert sand, thick oozing mud, steep rocky slopes or deep water.

The most successful vehicles for off-road racing are usually **four-wheel-drive** jeeps and trucks, although beach buggies and specially-made Volkswagen-powered racers also do very well.

USA

Ensenada

Mexico

La Paz

The Off-Road Racer

Like most other forms of motor sport, off-road racing has many different classes of racer, but they can be broken down into two basic types: the modified production vehicle (such as a Jeep or four-wheel-drive pickup truck), or a purpose-built single-seat racer. The most important quality they must have is rugged construction so that they can stand up to the punishing conditions.

A high ground clearance is essential. This prevents the chassis and floor hitting any bumps on the course and prevents the vehicle getting stuck on a narrow ridge, with all four wheels off the ground. For added protection a metal plate is fitted beneath the engine to prevent the oil pan being holed.

To ensure that the vehicle can cross loose or soft surfaces, special knobbly tyres are fitted, and many racers are equipped with powerful winches and strong cables so that if they do get stuck they can pull themselves free by

Right: Purpose-built single-seat racers with Volkswagen engines, such as this one, make good off-road cars.

passing the cable round a tree or boulder.

When travelling fast, it is not unusual for the off-road racer to leap into the air if it suddenly hits bumps or ridges. When it comes down it hits the ground very hard. Consequently, the suspension is always strengthened with stiffer springs and some extra shock absorbers. Sometimes cars come down so hard that they can lose a complete wheel assembly and have to continue on three wheels only.

When racing in really dusty desert conditions extra air filters have to be fitted to the carburettors to prevent the engine clogging up with sand, and as many endurance events run through the night plenty of spotlights must also be carried.

Protection for the driver and co-driver is also important, so a sturdy roll-over bar or complete cage is always fitted to the driving compartment. On long events extra water and emergency supplies are also carried.

The Racing Driver

Driving a racing car may look easy, but in reality it is very difficult to do successfully, requiring skill, courage, a lot of stamina and the ability to concentrate. In fact, a racing driver must be just as fit as a top athlete.

The driver in a Formula 1 Grand Prix race may have to drive the car at speeds of over 160 k/hr for as much as two hours non-stop, making 600–700 gearchanges. At the same time the cars are fighting with one another for position on the track. Iron nerves and quick reflexes are essential to take advantage of any situation to get closer to or even take the lead.

To make their task even more difficult the drivers are wrapped in several layers of flameproof clothing and sit in a cramped **cockpit** where the temperature may be as high as 50°C. In these conditions, a driver may lose as much as 4.5 kg in weight by sweating and is in serious danger of becoming dehydrated which will sap energy and slow down reactions.

So for any race it is essential that the driver is at the peak of fitness and that immediately before the start he drinks plenty of water or fruit juice to avoid the effects of dehydration.

Working with the Pit Crew

Another skill drivers must possess is the ability to understand how the car works. They should be able to explain to the pit crew chief any problems that might arise during the race so that the mechanics can put them right as quickly as possible.

The only way to success in motor racing is through teamwork. Although the driver actually does the racing, the pit crew chief and mechanics are responsible for making sure that the driver has a car capable of winning. Prior to any race they carry out many hours of track testing on each car in their team, altering tyres, suspension, brakes, steering, engine and bodywork until everything is perfect for the conditions they expect to race in.

During the race, the driver can keep in touch with the pit crew through a radio link in his helmet.

Below: Although the driver receives most of the glory for winning a race, it is very much down to teamwork.

Just as important is the pit crew chief who must make sure the car is running at peak performance.

Pit crew chief

Driver

Radio link

Flame-proof balaclava

Identity card

Sponsors' badges

Clipboard

Overalls

Crash helmet with radio link

Flame-proof overalls

Soft driving shoes

Safety on the Circuit

Motor racing has always been a dangerous sport for drivers, even in the very early days when the cars were not capable of travelling at any great speed. And despite tremendous improvements in car design and track safety facilities accidents do occasionally happen. So it is important that drivers are as well protected as possible, and it is a tribute to the safety measures taken that so few drivers are badly hurt in what can sometimes look like a very serious accident indeed.

One of the earliest safety measures taken by drivers was to wear a crash helmet instead of their usual head-gear of a soft cap or leather flying helmet. The crash helmet has changed shape considerably since it first appeared looking a bit like an upturned soup bowl! At first it was extended to protect the sides of the head and a peak was added to keep the glare of the sun out of the driver's eyes. Eventually, the full-face helmet appeared, providing protection for the whole head.

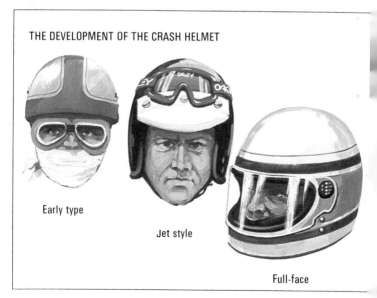

THE DEVELOPMENT OF THE CRASH HELMET

Early type

Jet style

Full-face

Early on, goggles were worn to protect the eyes but many drivers found that these restricted their vision and eventually the clear plastic visor was introduced which allowed them to see much more.

For a long time a helmet, some stout clothes and gloves was all the protection drivers had. But these did not stop them being flung from the car in a crash. This problem was solved by fitting safety harnesses with shoulder and lap straps which held the drivers in their seats. They also held them securely when the car raced round bends, making the job of controlling the car that much easier.

Above: A strong safety harness and stout roll bar ensure that the driver is protected in an accident. Notice how the straps of the harness go over both shoulders of the driver. They also come up across his lap to hold him firmly in his seat.

With drivers held firmly in their seats, it was essential to protect them in case the cars rolled right over. This was done by fitting a strong steel hoop, called a roll-over bar, behind the driver's head. On some cars a complete tubular steel cage is formed around the seat so that the driver is well protected in even the most destructive accidents.

In the Cockpit

Unlike the interior of a modern car, which is designed to be spacious and comfortable, the cockpit of a racing car is a very functional place with no unnecessary trim or fittings.

The cockpit of a Formula 1 racer, for example, will be very narrow – just wide enough for the driver to fit in. This allows the body of the car to be kept as narrow as possible to reduce wind resistance.

In front of the driver is a small panel containing the

Right: The driver of a Formula 1 car sits well forward in a tight-fitting cockpit.

Below: Here you can see just how cramped the cockpit is; it is fractionally wider than the driver's shoulders. You can also see the small steering wheel and the instrument panel.

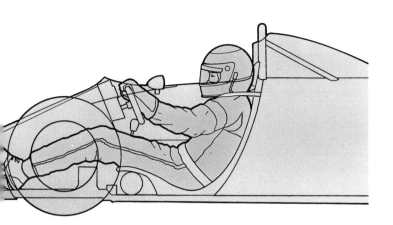

instruments which show how the engine is performing – water and oil temperature gauges, oil and fuel pressure gauges, a turbocharger boost pressure gauge and a tachometer (or rev counter) which indicates the speed at which the engine is turning in revolutions per minute. There is no speedometer. The driver is not bothered with the car's speed; the most important thing is to get into the lead by driving flat out.

A Formula 1 car will also have an ignition switch, a fuel pump switch, a turbocharger boost adjuster (adjusting the boost pressure varies the amount of total power the engine can give) and an engine fire extinguisher button. All of these will be mounted on either side of the instrument panel within easy reach of the driver when

strapped in. On the right-hand side of the cockpit will be a small gear lever and immediately in front of the instrument panel a small steering wheel.

When the car is built, the driver sits in it, in full racing gear, on top of a layer of clay which then forms to the shape of the driver's body. This clay mould is then used to make a tailored seat that will hold the driver firmly and comfortably in place throughout the race.

Most single-seater racing cars have similar cockpit layouts to the Formula 1 car.

Larger sports and saloon cars also have very functional cockpits with the same sort of equipment. But because they are bigger there is a lot more room inside and the driver is not quite so cramped.

Team Support

Competing in motor racing involves more than just a car and driver. For a driver to win a major motor race, there must be many people supporting his effort and they must have a large amount of equipment at their disposal. The higher the level of racing, the larger the team of people needed and the more equipment they need.

In Formula 1 racing, for instance, each team is run as a business and motor racing is the only job the team members do. Most teams do not do anything other than go racing and they are set up purely for this. However, some, such as Renault, are part of much larger car manufacturing firms.

Most teams will enter two cars in a Formula 1 Grand Prix, which means they must have two drivers to call on. Then they need a group of a dozen or so mechanics to look after those cars while they are at the circuit. The mechanics will have a very large kit of tools and will take with them large quantities of vital spare parts for the cars. These spares would include whole engines, body panels, brake and suspension parts, wheels and anything else that is likely to break or become damaged.

They will also carry radio equipment with them so that they can keep in touch with their drivers during the race.

Carrying two cars plus all this equipment presents a major problem, and most teams have large articulated transporter lorries which take everything from one track to the next. The lorries

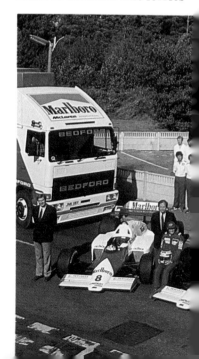

can act as mobile workshops for the teams and often have foldaway canopies on their sides which can provide shelter for the cars at night or during hot weather.

In addition to a transporter, each team will probably have a large motorhome in which they can eat their meals and which provides somewhere comfortable for the drivers to relax before the race starts.

Apart from the group at the circuit, the team is completed by the staff of the factory where the cars are constructed and by the designers and engineers who put them together.

As you can imagine, all this costs a lot of money, and teams solve this problem by sponsorship deals where large companies pay to have their name on the cars, the team equipment and the driver's overalls. Often, drivers have their own sponsors, which is why their overalls are covered with many different badges.

Below: It is surprising just how many people there are in a successful Formula 1 team. This is McLaren's.

The Pit Crew

An efficient pit crew is essential to the success of any racing car and driver. Not only do they make sure the car is running properly and correctly set up for the race, but they can make minor repairs and adjustments to it during the race. They also keep the driver informed of his position in relation to other cars, pass his lap times and also give advice or instructions from the team manager.

A Formula 1 Grand Prix pit crew may consist of 15 or more people, each of whom has a specific job to do. Most will be mechanics whose job it is to look after the cars.

In many races you will see cars making pit stops to change tyres. Often this can be essential if the weather conditions change during the race. If a car starts the race on dry weather tyres, for example, and it begins to rain, the car very soon becomes difficult to handle on corners, so wet weather tyres must be fitted.

When the car comes into the pits for a tyre change, the pit crew will be prepared with a new set of the right tyres already mounted on a

Above: Drivers are kept informed of their progress with a lap board. Notice the team manager's radio link to the car.

fresh set of wheels and positioned to allow a fast change.

As the car rolls to a halt, it is raised into the air by **hydraulic jacks** built into its chassis. Immediately, four members of the pit crew will remove all the old wheels, one man to a wheel, using pneumatic tools to undo and replace the retaining nuts. When each man has finished his job, he stands back and raises his arms in the air so that the pit crew chief can see exactly when to signal the driver that it is safe to rejoin the race. Once all four wheels have been replaced, the jacks are dropped and the car sprints away. A really well drilled pit crew can carry out this sort of tyre change in 10 seconds or less!

In particularly long races, the car's fuel tanks may be topped up during a pit stop, but this has been banned from Formula 1 events because of the danger of an accidental fire. All Formula 1 cars must now carry enough fuel to last the race.

Other members of the pit crew note their cars' lap times and also the times between their cars and the nearest other car in front of and behind them. They signal this information to the drivers with lap boards which have drop-in letters and numbers. The pit boards can also be used to tell the driver how many laps have gone, or how many there are left. They can also pass instructions to speed up, or slow down to conserve fuel.

Below: A complete tyre change in about 10 seconds! A well drilled pit crew make short work of this essential job.

Circuit Personnel

Organizing and running a motor race of any kind is a big job and a large number of people are needed on the day to carry out a wide variety of tasks to make sure it all goes smoothly. Many of them are unpaid, but highly skilled volunteers.

The Marshals

Many important jobs are done by the marshals who are usually stationed round the circuit in groups of two or three. They will be equipped with signalling flags and fire-fighting equipment. Their main jobs are to keep drivers informed of potential danger by means of the flags, to assist drivers in an emergency and keep the track clear. Some will be dressed in fireproof clothing so that in the event of an accident they can help free a trapped driver from a burning car.

Other marshals may be detailed to operate breakdown trucks or fire trucks, and yet more may be required to stop spectators getting on to the track. Although many

think the marshals are lucky in that they get a close up view of the racing, often they have to stand around for hours in the cold, the pouring rain or sweltering heat so they really earn their place next to the track.

Other Officials

Safety is of prime importance at any motor racing event, and the scrutineer has the job of inspecting all the cars before the race to make sure that they are both safely built but also that they comply with all the relevant rules and regulations. If he does not issue them with his

Above: Marshals are always ready with fire-fighting equipment to cope with accidents.

certificate, they are not allowed to race.

With safety in mind, there are always doctors and ambulances on hand at any motor race, again often volunteers.

Other important track personnel include the starter, who at one time used to wave a flag to start the race but now usually operates a set of traffic lights, and the timekeepers who note each car's lap times and race positions.

Flag Signals

At any motor racing event it is essential that drivers are warned of any dangerous situation ahead that they might not be able to see – an accident, oil on the track, etc. This is done by means of flag signals displayed around the circuit.

Various colours of flag are used, each colour having a different meaning, and when the driver sees a flag he knows just what to expect. If the flag is waved by a mar-shal it means that the danger is just ahead, but if it is stationary, the danger is a little way off.

The flags you will see have the following meanings:

Blue – another car is close behind or about to overtake.

White – a service car is on the circuit.

Yellow – danger, no over-taking, slow down.

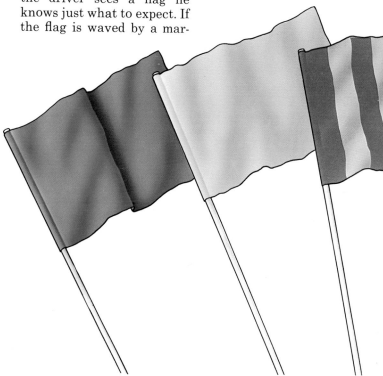

Left: Marshals use flags to warn drivers of danger on the track.

Yellow/red stripes – slippery surface ahead.
Green – track clear.
Red – stop racing.
Black – the race has stopped.
Black/white chequered – end of the race or finish.

Above: A selection of the different coloured flags you will see at a race meeting.

Famous Race Tracks

Motor racing is truly an international sport and the most well known series of races is the Formula 1 Grand Prix series. This takes place throughout Europe, America and South Africa on a wide variety of race tracks.

Some of the most famous circuits to be used for the Formula 1 Grand Prix are illustrated here.

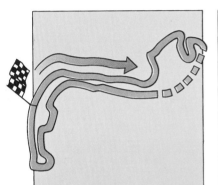

Monte Carlo

Until recently, the tight winding streets of Monte Carlo used to be closed off every year for the Monaco Grand Prix. Sadly they are no longer considered safe for this kind of racing.

The colourful circuit had a total length of 3.3 kilometres and an average Monaco Grand Prix consisted of 76 laps. Because the track twisted and turned, it put a great deal of strain on the cars and it also made overtaking difficult.

Paul Ricard

One of the newest racing circuits to be built, the 5.81-kilometre circuit was paid for by a millionaire, Paul Ricard, after whom it was named.

The circuit is well known for its long, sweeping straights which can put quite a strain on car engines.

When the French Grand Prix is held there the race normally lasts for 54 laps.

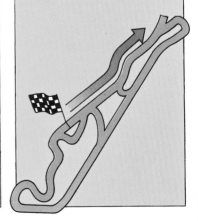

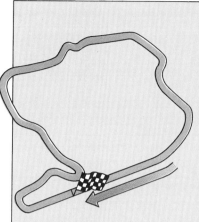

European track. It has a long straight that ends in a sharp right-hand hairpin bend, known as Tarzan bend. Because the cars reach such high speeds several really spectacular accidents have occurred here as cars are often unable to slow down sufficiently to get round it safely.

The Dutch Grand Prix normally comprises 72 laps of the 4.22-kilometre circuit.

Zandvoort
Home of the Dutch Grand Prix, this is another fast

Silverstone
One of the oldest motor racing circuits still in use in Great Britain, Silverstone becomes the home of the British Grand Prix every other year, alternating with another famous circuit, Brands Hatch.

Unlike many other circuits, the track does not twist and turn tightly but consists of a number of straights joined by relatively gentle bends. Its length is 4.67 kilometres.

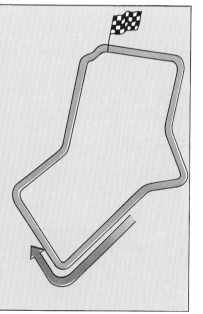

Glossary

Accelerator pedal This is operated by the driver's right foot to increase or decrease the speed at which the engine is turning to make the car go faster or slower. It is linked to the engine's carburettor or fuel injection system (see also these entries).

Aerodynamics The science of designing car bodies so that their shapes will move through the air with the least amount of resistance (see Wind resistance).

Aerofoil A device shaped like an aeroplane wing which provides a downforce to help keep the car on the track. Normally fitted to the front and rear of cars.

Aquaplaning Loss of driver control due to the car's tyres riding up on a layer of water when racing in wet weather.

Armoured hose Rubber fuel hoses covered in woven wire which protects them from accidental damage.

Banger A form of short-circuit racing car based on an old saloon car. Bangers are used in demolition derbies (see below).

Banked Sloping. Some oval circuits (like the old Brook-lands and Daytona) are built so that their track slopes upwards on bends. This allows cars to corner much faster than if the track was flat.

Brake horsepower (bhp) The measurement of an engine's power output. Most normal road-going family cars have engines of about 60–70 bhp.

Burnout Used in drag racing by drivers wishing to warm their rear tyres. The tyres are spun in puddles of water and friction heats them up.

Carburettor A device which mixes fuel and air before feeding it to the engine. It is linked to the accelerator pedal and used to vary the engine's speed.

Chassis A strong metal frame on which all the mechanical parts of the car are fitted and which carries the body.

Christmas Tree A traffic light system used for starting cars in drag racing events. So called because of all the coloured lights fitted to it.

Circuit A track sealed off from the public roads on which cars are raced.

Clutch This interrupts the flow of power from the engine to the gearbox, allowing the driver to pull away from a standstill and to change gear without stalling the engine.

Cockpit The driver's compartment of a racing car.

Combustion Chamber The part of an engine where the fuel is burnt to provide power. A piston below the combustion chamber is forced to move down a cylinder each time a fresh charge of fuel is ignited by a sparking plug. The piston is connected to a crank (like a bicycle pedal) which rotates as the piston moves. This rotation is passed to the gearbox and then the driving wheels.

Demolition derby A form of short-circuit racing where drivers are encouraged to smash into each other in bangers, the winner being the last one still moving.

Disc brakes A common form of braking system on racing cars. A solid metal disc is fitted behind the wheel and a caliper (like the brakes on a bicycle) sits over the top of the disc and clamps against it to apply the brakes.

Dragster A car specifically built for drag racing.

Ducting Tubing built into a racing car's body to channel air in a particular direction – usually to a radiator.

Elimination A knock-out system of racing pairs of cars in drag racing. The winners from each pair go through to the next round until only two are left in the final race.

Engine tuning Adjusting and modifying an engine so that it gives as much power as possible.

Floorpan The complete underside of a car.

Formula 1, 2, Ford, etc. A system of grading racing cars and the events they race in. Usually based on engine size and power or, in the case of Formula Ford, the mechanical components used to build the car. The Formula system is used in different types of racing: eg Formula 1 circuit racing cars are used in the Grand Prix series, but there are also Formula 1 stock cars which are totally different, racing on short circuits. In each case, the Formula 1 class is the highest class in that particular form of racing.

Four-wheel drive A system used mainly for off-road vehicles where all four wheels of the car are driven by the engine. Most road cars only have a pair of driven wheels.

Fuel injection A replacement system for the carburettor, which is much more efficient, allowing more power to be obtained from the engine. Rather than fuel being sucked in by the engine as with a carburettor, fuel is injected into the inlet by an electronically controlled pump.

Gearbox Fitted behind the engine and containing several gear wheels. The gearbox passes the power of the engine to the driven wheels and by selecting different groups of gears within the box, the driver can make the best use of the engine's power for pulling away, accelerating, slowing down, etc.

G-force The force of gravity acting against the driver's body when in a quickly accelerating or fast cornering car. It acts in the opposite direction to the movement of the body and the car.

Grand Prix Top race for Formula 1 circuit cars. An international series of Grand Prix races is held every year at circuits round the world.

Grid Starting area of a racing circuit where the cars are arranged ready for the start, normally side by side in pairs.

Hot rod A short-circuit racing saloon car.

Hub Part of the car's suspension that holds the road wheel and tyre. The hubs of the driven wheels are connected to the gearbox through the axle and driveshafts.

Hydraulic jack A means of raising and lowering a car so that wheels can be replaced, etc. Some racing cars have them built into their chassis, others need separate jacks.

Independent suspension A common form of springing on racing cars. Each wheel is attached to its own suspension unit which can move up and down independently of all the others. This sort of suspension gives good road holding.

Kart A very small one-man racing machine with · a motorcycle-type engine.

Lap board Used by pit crew to signal driver and supply information on his position in the race.

Monocoque A system of making a strong, rigid frame for a racing car without the need for a separate chassis. Monocoques are tubs made from folded sheet metal or other strong, lightweight materials.

Pace notes Notes used by a rally navigator to warn his driver of what to expect along their route.

Pits Service area at a racing circuit for racing cars. So called because of the trenches dug for service crews during the very early days of racing.

Qualifying sessions Take place before a race when cars are driven on the track against the clock. The times they record determine whether they are allowed in the race or not and their position on the starting grid.

Radiator Practically all car engines are water cooled. The water passes from the engine to the radiator where the heat is carried away by a flow of air passing through the radiator.

Rolling start A method of starting a motor race. Cars are assembled in their grid positions and are led round the track on a warm-up lap by a control vehicle. They have to keep their positions and are flagged away as they come round to the start line.

Roll-over cage A strong metal frame inside the car which stops the roof collapsing on top of the driver if the car rolls over in an accident.

Slick tyre A tyre with no tread used for maximum grip in dry weather racing.

Spoiler Fitted to the front of a car to force the air flow to the side to prevent a pressure build up below the car. Improves roadholding.

Stock car A purpose-built short-circuit racing car in Europe. A high-performance oval racing circuit saloon car in America.

Supercharger An engine-driven pump that forces fuel into the engine, allowing it to produce more power.

Tread Pattern of rubber blocks and grooves on the surface of a tyre which allows it to grip the road in the wet.

Turbocharger An exhaust gas-driven pump that forces fuel into the engine, allowing it to produce more power.

Wheelie Front wheels of a dragster coming right off the ground due to the rear tyres getting too much grip on the track at the start.

Wind resistance When a car moves forwards it has to part the air in front and this can take a lot of force, robbing the engine of some of its power. If the body is smoothly shaped it will part the air much more easily.

Index

Page numbers in *italics* refer to illustrations.

ERED by
ONDA
GOODYEAR
audia

Acknowledgements

Photographs: 10–11 BBC Hulton Picture Library; 16–17 L.A.T Photographic; 20 L.A.T Photographic; 21 John Townsend; 24–25 L.A.T Photographic; 26–27 Don Morley; 30–31 John Townsend; 32–33 BBC Hulton Picture Library; 35 Ford; 36 Chris Harvey; 40–41 Jim Crucefix; 42–43 Russell McCormack; 45 Chris Harvey; 46–47 J. Allan Cash Library; 50–51 top L.A.T Photographic; 51 bottom right Richard Nichols; 54 Richard Nichols; 57 Richard Nichols; 58–59 L.A.T Photographic; 60 Ford; 61 L.A.T Photographic; 65 Ford; 66 Talbot Motor Co Ltd; 75 John Townsend; 76 L.A.T Photographic; 78–79 John Townsend; 80 L.A.T Photographic; 81 John Townsend; 82–83 John Townsend; endpapers John Townsend.
Picture Research: Jackie S Cookson

Artwork: Eagle Artists, Rob Burns, Michael Roffe.

With thanks also to: ZIP Karts, Toleman Group Motorsport.